Rhino Life Lessons

32 Timeless Lessons to Achieve Strength, Wisdom, Confidence, and Resilience

CHRIS SWENSON, LMFT

DEDICATION

At first, I wanted to write a book for my kids that contained several lessons about life. I wanted to write these lessons down for them before something ever happened to me. I thought if I were to pass away what would I want my kids to know about life. So, I began collecting these life lessons in this book. Soon I realized that this knowledge and understanding has been given to me not to just pass on to my children, but to share with many others who could also pass on to their children.

LESSONS

ACKNOWLEDGMENTS

A special thanks goes out to Life for enrolling me in the school of hard knocks. Without that, I may not be writing these life lessons today. I am also forever grateful for the thousands of people who I have counseled over the years. Many of you have taught me many things about life that are also contained in this book. A special thanks goes out to those of you have been my greatest teachers and mentors. I am eternally grateful to all of you for your support and encouragement. I like to acknowledge my wife and kids for their support and encouragement as well. I have been blessed to be a part of an extended family where I grew up feeling loved. I give thanks to the Lord my God for creating me and giving me the gifts to write this book. I will continue to push on with the mission you have given me here on earth until you decide to call

INTRODUCTION

When you picked up this book you may have been wondering what this "rhino" stuff is all about. I mean the term life lesson is pretty clear and easily understood; but what is meant by rhino?

Quite possibly you may be wondering how you can achieve strength, wisdom, confidence, and resilience from an odd looking stubborn animal. In other words, what the heck can a rhino teach me about life as a human?

Well, the animal itself is not necessarily what I am talking about in this book. And no, I have never been an animal researcher that has studied the life of rhino's and now I want you to understand them. Rather, the term "rhino" is symbolic and means something very dear to me.

If you were to visually depict what my spirit looks like, it would be a rhino. To me, rhino equals powerful; in other words, a very powerful spirit. If I were to refer to you as a rhino, I am meaning you are powerful! Throughout the book you will read the term "rhino mentality" which literally stands for a powerful mentality or mindset.

What makes someone powerful? Powerful can be broken down into four components: strength, wisdom, confidence, and resilience. Strength isn't just representative of physical strength but also includes mental, emotional, and spiritual strength. Wisdom is the knowledge and understanding of yourself, others, and life. Confidence comes from faith in yourself, your teammates, and your higher power. Resilience is the ability to weather through anything that life throws your way.

With this understanding of what is meant by rhino, I want you to imagine yourself walking through the forest. As you are walking through the forest you begin to hear the sounds of birds singing and off in the distant you begin to hear the sound of running water. Soon you approach a pond and see a wooden dock. You walk over to the dock; take your shoes off, and while sitting on the edge you put your feet in the water.

Soon you begin reflecting about your life and come to a point where you feel all alone. You realize that your life has had many challenges and you haven't had that mentor type person to help guide you. Just then, someone else walks up right behind you and sits down next to you. You soon learn that this individual is a rhino; a very powerful, strong, wise, confident, and resilient individual. As the two of you begin to talk, this individual begins to share lessons about life with you. Those lessons are the thirty-two life lessons contained in this book.

As you read the lessons in this book, imagine having that strong, wise, confident, and resilient individual speaking to you directly. Each lesson may have more relevance to your life than others, but it is very important that after reading each lesson you reflect upon how that lesson impacts your life and how you can begin to apply what you learned. Only through this reflection and introspection will you be able to be on the road to becoming stronger, wiser, more confident, and more resilient.

The lessons in the book are not an exhaustive lesson on every aspect of life; however, they are very valuable. These lessons I have learned from the school of hard knocks, through counseling thousands of individuals, and learning from some great teachers. They are lessons that I continue to teach others with great results.

At first, I wanted to write a book for my kids that contained several lessons about life. I wanted to write these lessons down for them before something ever happened to me. I thought if I were to pass away what would I want my kids to know about life. So, I began collecting these life lessons in this book. Soon I realized that this knowledge and understanding has been given to me not to just pass on to my children, but to share with many others who could also pass on to their children.

The thirty-two life lessons are short and concise but not meant to be all read in one sitting. Rather, you can take one life lesson each day. Read it, and then begin to reflect and apply it to your life. As you continue with

2

this process, you may soon find yourself becoming stronger, wiser, more confident, and more resilient.

When you have completed the book, and you are looking for more life lessons. Simply check out my website http://rhinowellnesscenter.com or listen to the Rhino Mentality Podcast found on iTunes.

So, now is the time for you to begin the forest visualization again. As you imagine yourself sitting there with your feet in the water, the rhino has just appeared. Turn the page to Lesson One and begin the journey! Or, have a look at the table of contents, pick a lesson, and begin the journey!

LESSON ONE

WHAT YOU NEED TO KNOW ABOUT HITTING ROCK BOTTOM

THE WORLD IS ROUND AND THE PLACE WHICH MAY SEEM LIKE THE END MAY ALSO BE ONLY THE BEGINNING. – IVY BAKER PRIEST

1

WHAT YOU NEED TO KNOW ABOUT HITTNG ROCK BOTTOM

It can seem quite lonely and dim at rock bottom. You wonder why everyone else seems to be living a normal life and you just can't. It just doesn't seem fair!

There is no button that you can push to reset your life or your circumstances. However, soon you will come to find that hitting rock bottom is that reset button.

Two things that truly motivate people to make changes in their lives are inspiration and desperation….rock bottom serves as great desperation. Yes, a negative emotion is not all bad. Desperation is a very powerful energy and force that can be used to change your life for the better. The challenge is learning to direct that energy.

Where does this powerful energy come from during one of our darkest hours on earth? It actually comes from within! Even though you may feel like you have been stripped of everything around you, you have not lost the ever powerful energy of your spirit within you. Without considerable training, many of us are unable to tap into this energy without first having to hit rock bottom.

Being at rock bottom closely resembles being in a cocoon. Within this cocoon you are going through many painful changes that will eventually lead to shedding the cocoon and a birth of a new you!

You see, in that cocoon at rock bottom is life's blacksmith. The job of a blacksmith is to shape, create, and strengthen metal by heating it up and hammering it into shape. Take a moment to picture a blacksmith in your mind. Do you see them softening an odd generic looking metal piece by putting it into the fire? Then taking it out and hammering away at it? Do you see them repeating this process until finally cooling the metal by submerging it into water? In the end, they will use all sorts of tools to smooth out the edges creating that perfect looking item.

Life's blacksmith seeks to shape and create you, essentially leaving you stronger, wiser, and more resilient. However, the process can be painful. This process takes place within that cocoon at rock bottom.

Now once again picture that blacksmith. However, instead of working on metal, he is working on you! In that cocoon you will be put into the fire of life and it will burn; relax it is just softening you up. You will then be taken out of the fire and will get hammered away at. This pounding of life is difficult and tumultuous. If you are at rock bottom, you can truly relate to this pain and hammering from life and can feel exactly what I am talking about.

If you continue to press on and stay the course without giving up, eventually you will be cooled in the water of life and will begin to notice a more cooling down period. This period is where you begin to heal and recover.

However, you are not out of the woods yet. The finishing process of finalizing your shape, smoothing out your edges, and then polishing your new inner armor can still feel a bit raw. Trust me, stay the course and you will find that through this process you have become stronger, wiser, and more resilient!

If you don't finish the process, you will go through life unfinished, unformed, and with many rough edges. In a sense, you will continue on in life limping your way through the next trials. Those trials will be more difficult than they need to be because you are not as strong, wise, or resilient as you could be.

Going through the process essentially prepares and strengthens you for those next trials. In a sense, it is like the past trials have happened only to get you prepared for the next as you continue to advance through the levels of life learning and growing, becoming stronger, wiser, and more resilient.

There is no escape from the blacksmith of life. If you live long enough you will be dealing with that blacksmith over and over again. But with the proper mentality and successfully navigating the process you will continue to advance.

Simply put, hitting rock bottom can be a difficult time. However, it is not the end. Rather, it is a new beginning!

Many people every day serve as an inspiration to others because they too hit rock bottom and emerged from their cocoon a better person. Someone is going to lift themselves up from rock bottom and become an inspiration for others, why can't that person be you? Someone's going to do this, why not you?

LESSON TWO

COMMIT TO EXCELLENCE

EXCELLENCE IS THE GRADUAL RESULT OF ALWAYS STRIVING TO DO BETTER. – PAT RILEY

2

COMMIT TO EXCELLENCE

When I sat down to write this, I already knew what excellence meant to me and how a Rhino uses the word. However, I decided to see how Dictionary.com defined the word. Well, I was absolutely amazed and irritated at the same time, if that is possible.

Dictionary.com defined excellence as "the fact or state of excelling; superiority." I didn't have too many qualms with the first part of the definition, however the use of the word superiority definitely left me irritated as such a word isn't at all what I would use to describe excellence.

Excellence is not the same as superiority, to which I attach the word arrogance. A Rhino is not at all motivated or influenced by an air of superiority!

Excellence is about waking up each morning and declaring that you will do your best at everything you do and be better than you were the day before. Essentially it is all about growing, developing, learning, and getting better than you were before. To achieve superiority, you need to compare yourself to others. Excellence to a Rhino is a comparison to herself, not others. In other words, it doesn't matter what level your talents, abilities, or skills are currently at, what matters is whether you improve and get better! Improving and getting better than you were before is what a commitment to excellence is all about.

Legendary UCLA basketball coach John Wooden used this very concept when he was defining his pyramid of success. He indicated that while growing up his father had told him to always try to be the best that he could be and then let the results and comparisons take care of themselves. His father felt that such results and comparisons were out of his control and that focusing on doing his best was in his control. John Wooden eventually defined success as *"peace of mind which is a direct result of self-satisfaction in knowing you did your best to become the best that you are capable of becoming."* He taught this to his players at UCLA and they went on to win 10 National Championships in 12 seasons, including 7 straight. No other major college basketball team has ever come close matching that accomplishment.

Professional golfer, Jack Nicklaus held a very similar belief. Jack felt that he never competed against the other competitors at any event; rather he competed against himself and the course! He focused on playing the best he could against the course he was playing. Jack holds one of the most significant records in all of golf by winning 18 professional majors. No other golfer has been able to accomplish that feat.

Committing to excellence is what propels an ordinary person to create extraordinary success for themselves by waking up each morning and declaring that they will do their best at everything they do and work to be better than they were the day before.

When you enter the arena of life and start working to improve and get better each day, you will start meeting challenges, trials and tribulations, mistakes, and even failures. That's OK. A Rhino being influenced by excellence expects those challenges to take place and understands that those challenges will help her get better.

From a position of excellence, mistakes and failures are nothing but feedback needed to learn, grow, and get better! Never are they seen as negative events.

During those times, be on the lookout for three strangers who will seek to poison your mind and hijack your attempts to get better. Those evil strangers are complacency, perfectionism, and mediocrity.

LESSON THREE

STRESS: CONTROL AND USE; DON'T BE ABUSED AND DEBILITATED

STRESS SHOULD BE A POWERFUL DRIVING FORCE, NOT AN OBSTACLE. – BILL PHILLIPS

3

STRESS: CONTROL AND USE; DON'T BE ABUSED AND DEBILIATED

How many of you have ever heard the statement, "you need to remain calm in a demanding situation?" Have you ever been able to truly achieve a level of calmness in a stressful demanding situation? Me neither.

The truth is that in a demanding situation our body activates a stress level without us even thinking about it; a true psychological reflex. Basically, it's doing this so we can be poised to meet the demands of the situation. However, most of us struggle with controlling it and we quickly become abused and debilitated by the stress.

Research has shown that the right amount of stress will actually improve our ability to stay focused, more alert, heightens our five senses, and mobilizes strength and power to areas we need to meet the demand of the situation. This moderate level of stress actually improves our performance in stressful situations and even taking tests.

However, research also shows that our performance in meeting a demanding situation is greatly hindered when we are calm and virtually oblivious to the effects of the situation.

Too high of a stress level begins to breaks us down, immobilizing or freezing the body, leaving us dazed and confused, and reactive to the situation. Pretty much what happens is that blood flow stops going to the executive functioning in our brains and we are merely reduced to an animal or a caveperson. At that point, we are truly being abused and debilitated by our stress level.

Therefore, the next time you are facing a demanding situation, just remember you need to CONTROL AND USE the stress and NOT BE ABUSED AND DEBILITATED by it.

If you are not experiencing any stress you do not have the necessary energy and power needed to meet the demands. Virtually you may appear bored, tired, or unmotivated. You need to use your psychological skills to ratchet up stress to get into the sweet spot of moderate stress.

If you begin to be abused and debilitated by the high level stress, simply disconnect from what is stressing you by taking a break, then using your psychological coping skills and reduce the level of stress until you begin to get back into that sweet spot where your performance increases.

What is important to understand is that our heroes or those that appear calm under pressure are not actually feeling a sense of inner calmness, but rather are CONTROLLING AND USING the stress level to perform and face the situation. They seem to refuse to ever be   ABUSED   AND   DEBILITATED   by   stress!

LESSON FOUR

HOW STRESS IMPACTS OUR ABILITY TO MENTALLY PERFORM

*IT IS A MAN'S OWN MIND, NOT HIS ENEMY OR FOE, THAT
LURES HIM TO EVIL WAYS - BUDDHA*

4

HOW STRESS IMPACTS OUR ABILITY TO MENTALLY PERFORM

What happens to you when you become too stressed or too emotional? Quite simply, your biology kicks in and affects your ability to mentally perform. At some point you will experience this and knowing what happens and how to control it can save your relationships, jobs, and many other life experiences.

Once you become too stressed, the front part of your brain shuts down (the thinking and rational part of the brain which makes you human) and the back part or animal brain kicks-in (your animal part of the brain used for flight or fight responses, and reactivity). At the same time, your heart rate is increasing and chemicals (adrenaline and Cortisol) are being dumped into the blood stream preparing for fight or flight.

At the same time, your perceptions of situations are now impacted. You are prone to overreact, misjudge, and misinterpret what is happening. You may become on edge, jumpy, defensive, and tense. You are no longer able to truly listen to a person you are talking to.

Rather, you are too focused on what to say next or just plain focused on yourself. You will have developed tunnel vision and may be striving to prove your point just to be right. Your insecurities will begin to enter the picture and further cloud your perceptions and judgments and most likely will be speaking for you!

At this point, you are truly emotionally intoxicated and your ability to mentally perform is greatly hindered! Continuing in this state of mind will only create further complications in the world around you and your relationships with others.

This process can happen whenever your mind perceives a potential threatening situation and even when you are overwhelmed. Whether the situation is real or not doesn't matter as whatever you present to the mind you will feel. In other words, you can simply imagine a stressful situation in your mind, and this process will begin! Your insecurities are great at doing this.

So, how do you gain control of yourself during times of high emotions, stress, or being overwhelmed? You can't fight biology. If you think you can, then the next time you have to go to the bathroom try to hold it and see how successful you are! You need to use two steps to work with the biology to regain control:

Step One: Get control of your biology!

To do this, you will need to engage in deep breathing. Deep breathing, if done correctly, will successfully reduce your heart rate and therefore begin to reverse the biological process described above and you will have a return to normal functioning.

Usually, you have developed tunnel vision as well. To reduce the tunnel vision, simply focus on your peripheral vision while breathing. This will help slow down your perceptions.

Step Two: Control the "Monkey Mind"

If you don't seek to control your mind, then your monkey mind will take control and will run from topic to topic continually until you are overwhelmed or feel like you are going crazy! You need to put the brakes on this mind train being driven by a monkey.

To do this, you will need to begin to direct your mind (using your five senses) to think about and focus upon what is happening in the present moment; this is called being mindful. Begin to notice and describe what you see. Next, what do you hear? What do you smell? If you are eating something, notice its taste and smell. Can you feel the chair you are sitting on? Or, can you feel the ground under your feet. Begin to notice your breathing, feeling it going in and out.

Basically, you are being highly focused upon what is going on around you right in the moment and not thinking about what happened or what is going to happen. Stay in the moment!

If all else fails, don't worry because even if you don't do anything, your monkey mind will at some point begin to think about something else thus distracting you and getting the train to switch tracks.

Both steps are not easy to do during difficult times and definitely require practice! Begin today to use these two steps to help you navigate whatever your day may bring to you.

LESSON FIVE

NEED EMOTIONAL RELIEF? YOU GOTTA TRY THIS!

PAIN IS INEVITABLE. SUFFERING IS OPTIONAL. – M KATHLEEN CASEY

5

NEED EMOTIONAL RELIEF? YOU GOTTA TRY THIS!

How many times do you feel yourself struggling with stress or feeling worried? If you are like many Americans, you may feel like such feelings are normal and may have no idea how actually stressed you really are.

Stress and worry can feel absolutely miserable and painful. However, how we respond to, or deal with our stress and strain can lead to even more pain. Engaging in gimmicks and unhealthy measures to alleviate our stress and strain only breaks the body down leaving us more vulnerable to stress than before! That alcoholic drink to unwind and loosen up works in the moment, but breaks us down leaving us more sensitive the next day to strain. So what do we do? Drink more again! Doesn't that sound strange?

Buddha once asked a student, "If you are struck by an arrow, does that hurt?" The student responded, "Yes." The Buddha then asked, "If you are struck by a second arrow, does that hurt more than the first?" The student then replied, "Yes." Buddha then explained that what happens to you (the circumstances) is the first arrow. The second arrow is your response to the first arrow!

The stress and strain of your day is nothing but the first arrow. Yes, you will feel some sort of uncomfortableness and pain from the circumstances, but you must resist responding to the day by striking yourself with a second arrow! Unhealthy coping may work in the short run to feel better, however such choices will leave you weakened and more susceptible to stress the next day!

There is a real simple answer to this problem. Have you ever taken a sigh of relief? You know that deep inhale and strong exhale that leaves you feeling RELIEF (which is why they call it a sigh of RELIEF). Yep, that is it! All you need to do is take a few sighs of relief and you will soon feel much better. Oh and you will not actually deplete yourself for the next day. Sometimes it may take a few of those sighs but, it is much better than any gimmick or unhealthy coping mechanism.

To do this, you need to inhale through the nose and fill up your lungs from the stomach up, not the chest down. While doing this inhale, you can visualize sucking up all that stress and strain, pulling it together and waiting to exhale it out of you. Then, exhale out the mouth and expel all that garbage and strain while relaxing your tense muscles. That's it!

Many of you have already breathed a sigh of relief at some point, so using it when feeling stressed or even worried can be a simple, healthy response that leaves you feeling RELIEF! Plus, you are not striking yourself with a second arrow because you are not weakening yourself for the next day, rather you are strengthening and recovering for the next the day!

Now that you have been made aware of this, the choice is yours! When struck by that first arrow of circumstance, how are you going to respond?

LESSON SIX

STOP MARINATING IN YOUR PAIN AND SUFFERING

ONE OF THE MOST HEALING THINGS YOU CAN DO IS RECOGNIZE WHERE IN YOUR LIFE YOU ARE YOUR OWN POISON. – STEVE MARABOLI

6

STOP MARINATING IN YOUR PAIN AND SUFFERING

When you are hungry you go and look to cook something to satisfy your hunger. You may choose some type of meat and seek to marinate the meat to add flavor. Marinating the meat involves allowing the meat to soak in a marinating sauce for a specified amount of time. This marinating sauce is composed of acidic ingredients that soften the meat allowing the flavor to soak in.

What the heck does marinating meat have to do with your life? Well, read on and I will do my best to illustrate.

The secret ingredient needed to develop strength and wisdom is *responsibility*. Responsibility is merely being accountable for your own actions and choices. The only way to obtain strength and wisdom is by being truly responsible for your life.

You are NOT responsible for everything that happens to you. Rather, you ARE responsible for DEALING with what happens to you.

If you wish to become strong and resilient in life (a Rhino), then you must accept accountability and responsibility for your choices/responses to what has happened to you. In other words, the road to being resilient starts with a choice, the choice to take responsibility and not look to escape it.

If you take responsibility for your life, then you become not a victim, but a Rhino. A victim will fall prey to fear, enjoy blaming, and lead a life of denial. The Rhino creates his own path which may be more challenging and difficult, but much more rewarding.

Your desire to avoid responsibility can be overwhelming at times. Just remember, if you choose a path of victimhood (denying accountability), you will forever marinate in your pain and suffering and lead a life of excuses, blame, self-pity, whining, weakness, cowardice, and a defeated spirit.

Essentially, not taking responsibility creates a chronic marinating sauce for you to become softened and flavored for the evil of our world. There is no way out of your pain and suffering when you deny accountability and responsibility for your life.

Your response to what happens to you determines which choice you make. If you find yourself responding with excuses, blame, self-pity, whining, or denial, then you have truly denied responsibility. Get ready to marinate in your pain and suffering and wishing things would be different.

The alternative choice is to accept responsibility by moving through the pain and suffering, fear and tragedy, so that you can learn and grow thus becoming wiser and stronger (more resilient). Remember, you are NOT responsible for EVERYTHING that happens to you. Rather, you ARE responsible for DEALING with what has happened.

Decide to move through and face what has happened and you grow stronger and wiser becoming more and more resilient. Or, choose to hide, run-away, deny, blame, offer excuses, and you will forever marinate in your pain and suffering. The choice is yours. What choice do you want to make?

If you decide to face the darkness of what has happened, never seek to do that alone. No need to face the darkness alone, seek out support from family, friends, or other professionals. That way the odds of your success go way up!

LESSON SEVEN

DON'T EVER FACE DARKNESS ALONE

A MAN'S PRIDE CAN BE HIS DOWNFALL, AND HE NEEDS TO LEARN WHEN TO TURN TO OTHERS FOR SUPPORT AND GUIDANCE – BEAR GRYLLS

7

DON'T EVER FACE DARKNESS ALONE

You are about to go on a journey that you didn't ask for. This journey will be to a place that is dark, scary, and painful. On this journey you will experience some intense emotions, you may feel helpless, and at times you may wonder if there is any way out. This place will saturate you with negativity, bring forth nearly every fear you have, and get you to question your very existence. After this experience you will never be the same again.

If you so choose, you can go and experience this journey alone. Or, you can bring with you as many friends and family members as you wish to help you. In addition, to your family and friends, you can also choose to bring with you a guide that has helped others successfully walk this journey and possesses the wisdom to give you some suggestions or cheats when on this journey.

So, what do you choose? Go at it alone? Or, face it with family, friends, and a guide? Nearly every person I ask this to answers with, "face it with family, friends, and definitely that guide." This question is purely hypothetical and obviously most people would choose that option. However, what happens when this is no longer hypothetical, but real.

Interestingly, once the experience is real many individuals who initially said they would bring supports and a guide begin to face the darkness alone! Many more may have brought their family and friends, but never choose the guide!

You will face this darkness at some point in your life, and quite possibly numerous times. This darkness journey will appear when you are suddenly faced with the death of a loved one, a nasty divorce that you didn't ask for, trauma, tragedy, and during many of your most painful experiences.

These circumstances in your life bring with it the black rain of life that rains down, creating darkness, and soaking you in emotional pain and turmoil. The darkness begins to cut you off from your family, friends, and other supports, isolating you away from others. It will convince you that asking for their assistance will only burden them, and how weak you are for asking for help because you can do this on your own. Before you know it, you are on that journey through darkness all alone.

The key lesson here to remember is to never face darkness alone! There is no need to. If you bring supports the odds of your success go way up. If you bring with you your supports and a guide your odds of success skyrocket!

So the next time you are facing the darkness of life's circumstances, remember don't allow it to cut you off from your supports. Immediately begin to plug yourself in with your support network and hang on to them tightly as this journey can be quite rocky.

Who is this guide? That guide would be a counselor that possesses the knowledge and wisdom to get through these trials and tribulations of life. A counselor, who will walk with you through this darkness and give you the necessary wisdom and tools to successfully navigate the waters of this dark journey.

Just remember, the darkness will do whatever it can to get you to believe that seeking out counseling is wrong, so be on alert. Pay attention to your thoughts about going to counseling. Are they really yours, or quite possibly they could be the darkness trying to get you to choose to go at this alone! Going at darkness alone is not a measure of strength, it is a measure of stupidity.

The choice is always yours. What are you going to choose?

LESSON EIGHT

PSYCHOLOGICAL GPS TECHNOLOGY

HE WHO HAS A WHY TO LIVE CAN BEAR ALMOST ANY HOW.
– FRIEDRICH NIETZSCHE

8

PSYCHOLOGICAL GPS TECHNOLOGY

Many times throughout your life you will deal with stress and the struggles of life. There will be events in your lifetime that will hit so hard you will end up spiraling out of control, eventually feeling the pain of being knocked down, and left feeling broken and shattered.

It is during these hard dark times that you will be left dazed and confused about how to get out of this mess and back in the fight of life.

Having a Rhino mentality, or simply being a Rhino, doesn't make you immune to the stress and struggles of life. Rhino's also experience those dark times, however, they seem to have an internal compass (an internal GPS) that provides a light during these times of darkness.

That internal GPS is their sense of purpose which provides a sense of direction during the darkest of times. Once you are able to develop your purpose in life, you will now be armed with the latest in psychological GPS technology!

Without a sense of purpose, life's darkest events will knock you around like a pinball bouncing around out of control. However, with a sense of purpose, you are now poised to utilize the pounding and shifting to send you hurling even faster towards your purpose.

Rhinos are people who understand that dark moments in life do not need to be debilitating. Rather, they USE the event to make them stronger and wiser which leads them closer to their purpose.

They seem to heal and recover with a sense of purpose. There is a difference between just healing and recovering and healing and recovering with a sense of purpose and direction.

Healing and recovering without a purpose is the epitome of the pinball experience described above.

Healing with a sense of purpose allows you to find meaning in the struggle, to understand that all the blows and pounding are constantly forging and molding you to be a better person. Plus, when you do heal and recover (and you will) you will now be stronger and wiser to really take on life and get back in that fight again!

How do you develop your purpose? Your purpose essentially is the "why" of your life. It describes what is important to you and what kind of person you want to be.

Go ahead, take a risk, and sit down to write your purpose today. Maybe you will describe the purpose in a few sentences or maybe a few paragraphs. Just remember, YOUR purpose must be YOURS not someone else's. In other words, it must be an intrinsic motivating purpose (from inside of you) that is meaningful and moving for you.

Over time, you will adjust some of the wording as you grow and change; so don't write it in concrete unless you want to be stuck in there with them.

Connecting to your purpose is the first step in being able to show resiliency and strength in the face of dark times. So don't delay, begin to uncover your purpose today!

LESSON NINE

HOW TO BEAT DEPRESSION

*TEARS, IDLE TEARS, I KNOW NOT WHAT THEY MEAN, TEARS
FROM THE DEPTHS OF SOME DIVINE DESPAIR – ALFRED
LORD TENNYSON*

9

HOW TO BEAT DEPRESSION

Depression silently enters the room unannounced and uses its sticky fingers to tighten its grip upon its victim. The victim, unaware of depression's presence, begins to feel sad and starts to withdraw or isolate from others just falling right into depression's hands and the grip is tightened.

Once feeling down and isolated, depression begins to take away the victim's energy and motivation, eventually getting them to see and think about all the crap in their life, introduces thoughts to harm themselves, and other dark thoughts. The victim unaware of the tightening grip becomes immobilized and dances right into the plans of depression.

If you have ever battled with depression, then you may be all too familiar with the above scenario. It seems that no matter what you try to do, depression is right there commanding every move and tightening its grip.

However, there are some secrets that can be used to really tick off depression and loosen its grip and leave you in control. A few of them are listed below.

Movement
Depression does not like movement; it needs for you to be immobilized so it can continue to mess with you. Get up and move around, dance to music, go for a walk, take a hike, etc. Whatever you do, you really need to move and break free of the grip!

This is usually easier said than done and anyone battling depression can agree. Have you ever had the feeling when you got up and moved that you just don't feel like it? Or, when you are doing something you get the thought that it just isn't working?

Depression becomes angry when you move and will work very hard to use your thoughts to get you to stop. That is what is happening when you have those feelings (it isn't working, I don't feel like it, etc....). You really need to keep doing it and fight through those feelings and thoughts because eventually, they will release the grip of depression. It may not take away the depression but, it will loosen the grip.

This mental battle is what I call the Mental Game of Depression because depression uses your thoughts and feelings to control you. Your mind is the battlefield and if it wins, it tightens the grip. However, when you win, you loosen the grip and take back control.

Body Language
Depression needs you to walk, talk, and act a certain way so it can easily mess with you. Picture a person struggling with depression and what do you picture? Can you see how they may be walking slower, head down, laying around, crying, speaking monotone and slower speech?

In a way, depression is like a movie director getting you (its actor) to act in a certain way for its benefit. The way to take back control is to become your own movie director and get yourself to act in the opposite. Smile, keep your head up, walk faster, etc. What you want to do is direct yourself to act like a person who is happy.

Once again, when beginning to do this you may hear thoughts like: "This is stupid," "This isn't going to work," "I am not happy why act like it," and many more such thoughts. When you hear and feel these statements, it is just depression whining like a little baby trying to get its way with you again. As noted earlier, depression needs you to act a certain way so it can mess with you. When you don't do this, it needs to convince you to stop and go back to behaving like it wants.

People
Depression needs for you to be isolated and not around a bunch of people because it is easier to mess with you when you are alone. Abusive people are much like depression, they need you to be away from those that will help and if they can get you alone, look out!

When you feel the grip of depression trying to convince to withdraw and be alone, be sure to get out of the house and be with people. Try to contact a friend, call a hotline, go to the store, go shopping, watch people in a park, just do something to avoid being alone with depression.

When you begin to do this or even think about doing this, depression will try to convince you not to go. You will have similar thoughts of not wanting to be around others, thoughts like "no one cares," and "who would want to be around me anyways."

The bottom line is for you to resist the grip of depression in any way you can, then resist the mental games depression is playing with you when you start resisting! I know that this is easier said than done but, you can do it

It is very important for you to contact a loved one, friend, 911, your local emergency room, hotline, or a mental health professional if the grip of depression has become very difficult to resist and you are having thoughts of hurting or killing yourself.

The mental game of depression is a difficult one but, it can be won. Consistently resisting the grip is your way to take back control of your life and feel better.

There are certainly many more secrets to battling depression. If you like to learn more, then check out the **Dealing with Depression episode** on the **Rhino Mentality Podcast**.

LESSON TEN

THE ONE KEY TO MENTAL DURABILITY

*A GOOD LAUGH AND A LONG SLEEP ARE THE BEST CURES
IN THE DOCTOR'S BAG – IRISH PROVERB*

10

THE ONE KEY TO MENTAL DURABILITY

How often have you become worn out as the day goes on? Or, worse yet, are already worn out even before the day has begun?

The term "durable" can be defined as capable of withstanding wear and tear. When we apply this term to our mental fortitude, we can define "mental durability" as the ability to withstand the wear and tear of the day or life itself.

The one key to achieving mental durability is sleep. It is vitally crucial for your ability to withstand the wear and tear of the day that you get at least 7-8 hours of sleep per night. However, that number may vary depending on your own individual needs. What you are after is being able to wake up, feel refreshed, and alert for the day.

Many of us adults understand the effects upon a young child or baby that is quite irritable due to feeling tired. However, we seem to ignore that same principle when applied to ourselves.

When facing even a small amount of sleep deprivation your mental performance is impacted. You tend to have difficulty sustaining attention, loss of focus, slowed response, difficulty with all facets of memory and recall, and your ability to cope with the day is greatly diminished. Even the slightest of difficulties can become like a mountain for you to overcome.

There are four things you can do to improve the quality and quantity of your sleep:

1. Stick to a sleep schedule
2. Pay attention to what you eat and drink
3. Regular exercise
4. Manage stress

There are many other things you can do to improve the quality and quantity of your sleep. If you are interested, engage in a search on the internet and become educated about sleep.

LESSON ELEVEN

THE POWER OF FOCUS AND HOW IT DIRECTS YOUR LIFE

THE MOMENT ONE GIVES CLOSE ATTENTION TO ANY THING, EVEN A BLADE OF GRASS IT BECOMES A MYSTERIOUS, AWESOME, INDESCRIBABLY MAGNIFICENT WORLD IN ITSELF – HENRY VALENTINE MILLER

11

THE POWER OF FOCUS AND HOW IT DIRECTS YOUR LIFE

Ever watched a scary movie? If so, can you remember some of those scary scenes that just freaked you out or made you jump? How did the producer of that movie get you to do that! Well, the producers utilize certain camera angles that direct your focus upon what the producer wants you to focus upon. Then will bring in some suspense music that further drums up certain emotions in you. If the producer is successful, you will feel that emotion quite intensely!

Well, what does movie producers have to do with life? Everything!!! You see, your eyes are a camera that visually soaks up whatever your mind (producer) tells it to. Whatever you focus upon is what you pay attention to and dominates what you may be experiencing, while everything else going on is drowned out. A key phrase to remember is, "whatever you focus upon is what is most real to you."

Whatever you focus your attention on and how you interpret what is going on determines how you feel. For example, a young man came into my office for help because he felt he may be depressed. He reported that pretty much everywhere he goes it doesn't seem like he or anyone else is having a good time.

After a great deal of questioning, we narrowed down the struggle. Each time he would enter a party; he focused his eyes upon those sitting in the corners and having no fun and soon began to feel like he wasn't having any fun either. When he began thinking back, he realized that there was a great deal of other people at the party but, wasn't sure what they were doing because he didn't focus upon them.

He went to another party and decided to explore what those other people may be doing and find out what he may be missing; kind of his own experiment. He soon found out that he began having more fun and was meeting more people.

What was the difference? He chose to focus upon those having fun and interacting at the party instead of those sitting in the corner bored! His camera (eyes) presented his mind with different scenes that evoked a new feeling. He just needed to control that focus better.

Try this right now. Find an object in the room you are sitting in right now. Focus on that object. You will notice that object as being clear, in color, and bright and vivid. Now, shift your focus to the right where you can still notice the object but, this time the object is now in your peripheral vision. You will find that what you are focusing on now is clear, in color, bright, and vivid, and everything else around it is blurred! Any object in the blur you can make clear by shifting your focus to it. But, when you do that, you will blur out the rest.

So, if you don't like what you are experiencing, then why continue to focus upon that? As you now know, as you focus on it, it becomes more real, and more vivid, therefore creating a certain emotion within you. Change your focus to something else and then that becomes more vivid, real, and may create a different emotion within you.

Go out today and give it a try. Also, begin to pay attention to what you focus your camera (eyes) on quite often during the day. Shift the focus and begin to experience something different!

LESSON TWELVE

THE TRUTH ABOUT COUNSELING YOU NEED TO KNOW

EVERYONE THINKS OF CHANGING THE WORLD, BUT NO ONE THINKS OF CHANGING HIMSELF. – LEO TOLSTOY

12

THE TRUTH ABOUT COUNSELING YOU REALLY NEED TO KNOW

Many people assume that if they go to counseling they will somehow be viewed as "weak," "incapable of solving problems on their own," or are just plain "crazy." Others are afraid that they may be seen as "worthless, flawed, or unlovable."

When did going to get help become a serious attack on one's character? I don't know about you, but the problems of our world must love these beliefs! Namely because they prevent people from getting help and feeling better which allows the problem to continue to get worse and make more problems for people.

The truth…People who go to counseling improve **four times as much** as those who do not seek counseling. This has been scientifically proven over and over and over again! Yet, people continue to decide to not seek help, continue to wallow in their suffering, and continue to struggle.

Research has also shown counseling to be more effective than aspirin and just as effective as brain surgery and gastric bypass! Clearly, counseling works!

I don't know about you, but suffering and struggling are two things I really don't enjoy. Even more ludicrous is choosing to continue to suffer and struggle despite knowing a solution that may help!

Oh, I understand… it is tough struggling and suffering, but going to counseling may result in being seen as "crazy" or "inferior," and you wouldn't want that! (Stated sarcastically)

If only you could get a glimpse of who really goes to counseling, then you probably wouldn't have so many issues with going.

The reality is the majority of people who go to counseling are **ordinary, everyday people dealing with ordinary, everyday problems!** They have serious life challenges or are going through difficult life transitions that may be taxing their ability to cope. These challenges may be adversely affecting their ability to function at a level they desire.

Examples of such challenges: work-related stressors, career issues, financial problems, health issues, stress, family or parent/child conflicts, academic issues, death of loved ones, relationship breakups, divorce, relationship struggles, and major life decisions related to life choices. Others are simply seeking to grow and become better as a person. Or, are just not sure of what to do and have noticed their way of reacting is creating more problems.

These are just some of the reasons why people decide to go to counseling. So, if you are going through one or more of these challenges at the same time, you're not alone. The effects are often cumulative, which is generally referred to as a "pile-up" of stressors. Counseling during these times can be quite helpful in providing both the support and skills to better address these life challenges.

You see, **ordinary, everyday people dealing with ordinary,**

everyday problems! The idea that people seeking help for normal, common issues are somehow flawed couldn't be further from the truth! The truth is going to counseling is **an invaluable investment** in your emotional, physical, and mental health, **an act of courage not weakness**, and **a gift** to those whose lives you touch each and every day.

LESSON THIRTEEN

WHAT YOU NEED WHEN YOU FACE DARKNESS

RHINO MENTALITY IS THE POWERFUL INNER ARMOR YOU NEED TO WEATHER THROUGH ANYTHING IN LIFE. – CHRIS SWENSON

13

WHAT YOU NEED WHEN YOU FACE DARKNESS

Every day and every challenge we face, we are under attack by the constant barrage of Darkness' black rain of abuse chipping away at our psyche. It is that little voice in your head that guilt trips you, leaves you feeling confused, lost, questions your very existence, gets you to feel worthless, and constantly criticizes your every move.

Darkness is the greatest enemy you will face in your life. Aside from the mind games noted above, it gets you to hesitate and procrastinate on your dreams, isolates you from your supports, questions your level of commitment to your dreams, sends fear racing through your veins, and impedes your ability to succeed every day of your life.

Whenever you set a goal for yourself, it is there. Whenever you seek out to obtain your dreams or pursuit of something important to you, it is there. When you face a trauma or a tragedy in life, it is there. Darkness is your opponent on the field of life working to prevent you from winning at life.

When you face darkness it will seek to get you to adopt a negative mentality, or mindset. This negativity will spiral you out of control, eat away at your soul, and leave you feeling doubtful, weak, and scared. Then, you will look to quit or find a way out. Once again it has prevented and controlled your life and stolen your dreams.

Having a Rhino Mentality is your armor against Darkness' black rain of negativity penetrating your soul. Having a Rhino Mentality is everything. With it you take risk, face adversity, accept failure, and embrace your fears. Without it, you are controlled and held captive by Darkness.

You combat all types of fears with a Rhino Mentality. With a Rhino Mentality you are able to accept the never-ending struggles associated with life. In case you haven't figured it out already, life is tough. We all face challenges and Darkness; some more than others.

A Rhino Mentality begins with a positive attitude. Are you more often a negative or positive person? Most people give the social desirable response and report that they are mostly positive. However, when we observe people's actions, we see quite the opposite.

The foundation of your positive attitude relies on your ability to look at life as a gift and opportunity to grow stronger, wiser, and more resilient. Keep in mind, a Rhino Mentality can never be forged with a negative attitude.

The key to remember is that Darkness' black rain of negativity erodes your armor (Rhino Mentality) protecting your soul. Pay attention to how much this negativity surrounds your own conversations, self-talk, and the people you surround yourself; especially when you seek out to advance your life. Awareness is the first step towards any change.

Just remember, the next time you are faced with a challenge, you will be toe to toe with Darkness and its black rain of negativity. So do whatever it takes to fight to keep your positive attitude and see how much better you weather the challenge. Or, you can focus on the negative and try to complain and whine your way to success; which will never happen!

If you would like to learn more about a Rhino Mentality, then check out my Rhino Mentality website and Podcast.

LESSON FOURTEEN

A POWERFUL STORY OF CHANGE

WE MUST EMBRACE PAIN AND BURN IT FOR FUEL FOR OUR JOURNEY – KENJI MIYAZAWA

14

A POWERFUL STORY OF CHANGE

Many years ago I had counseled an individual that told me a truly powerful story. I would love to share that story with you now. As you read the story, pay attention for certain kind of life lessons, or golden takeaways from what you are about to read.

I have changed the name of the individual to protect his privacy and identity. Here goes the story…

Bill was at rock bottom. The darkness of life had been hammering away at him constantly, or it seemed that way. His wife and three children had been killed in a car accident, he was laid off at his job, his home was about to go into foreclosure, and if that wasn't enough, he also was recently diagnosed with cancer.

Many days Bill felt tired, defeated, and worn down from the hammering of life. However, this particular day was rough. No matter what he tried, he just couldn't shake the pain, and depression running through his veins. Suicidal thoughts were running through his head like a broken record player playing over and over and over again. He was losing control and he knew it.

Without even wanting to, Bill was planning to kill himself. However, just at this very moment Bill heard something outside of his house that would forever change the course of his life.

He heard a constant high pitched yelping from the backyard. For some reason, the pain, depression, and suicidal thoughts were interrupted by this sound. He felt compelled to go into the yard and see what was going on.

In the back yard, he found an unknown dog that was pinned under a tree branch that must have fallen. The dog apparently was injured from the branch falling on him and then was trapped under the weight.

Bill could see the pain and fright in the poor dog's eyes. The yelping were sounds of crying out for help. Immediately, Bill freed the dog from under the tree branch and took the dog inside to safety and decided to nurse the dog back to health. What Bill did not know, was that decision would forever change the course of his life.

Bill's focus and purpose was now on helping that dog. As time wore on, the dog healed and a very strong friendship between the dog and Bill had formed.

After several days and a couple of months of this, Bill noticed that his own pain had lessened in intensity and frequency. The constant hammering of suicidal thinking had ceased. He began to feel some life in him again, motivation began to return, and Bill found strength to once again face his circumstances and crawl out of this dark hole.

Bill went on to make a full recovery, or what could be considered a full recovery given his unfortunate circumstances. Both the dog and Bill seemed to heal up together.

What kind of life lessons can you take from this story? Take some time to think.

One lesson you can take is that when you are going through a great deal of pain, get your eyes (focus) off of you and your pain. Then place them upon helping others or making a difference in the life of someone else.

Beginning to take any sort of action in that direction will begin to re-light a fire in you. You too will soon find your motivation will return and that strength to push on. Now that doesn't happen immediately, but with constant effort in the direction of helping others or helping a good cause will eventually re-set the negative feelings.

Remember, never face darkness alone. Seek out your supports and the help of a trusted counselor along the way. Bill did just that, and he began to fight for his life, instead of fighting against his life. He didn't do that alone, he had support.

LESSON FIFTEEN

HOW TO TAKE CONTROL OF THAT EMOTIONAL ROLLER COASTER

FEELINGS ARE MUCH LIKE WAVES, WE CAN'T STOP THEM FROM COMING BUT WE CAN CHOOSE WHICH ONES TO SURF – JONATAN MARTENSSON

15

HOW TO TAKE CONTROL OF THAT EMOTIONAL ROLLER COASTER

When riding on a roller coaster you do not have any way of controlling or steering the ride. Pretty much all you can do is just hang on as you are at the mercy of the ups and downs.

I hear many of us describe our emotional life like that of a roller coaster ride. In fact, it is true that we are going to have many ups and downs; however, we do have ways to steer that ride so we don't have to make the ups and downs more worse than they already are.

That steering wheel is our self-talk and our ability to direct our mind. Your thoughts are like a vehicle driving your emotional life. In fact, many studies have shown that we have about 50,000 thoughts per day! We are thinking all the time, but may not be aware of it.

A single thought releases chemicals in your brain that trigger an emotional impulse that can run throughout your body. That emotional impulse that you feel is your emotions. Simply put, you have a thought, and then you have an emotion.

Try this right now. Imagine putting a lemon in your mouth. Now notice what happens. Is your mouth beginning to salivate? Yes! You see your mind doesn't know the difference between what is really happening and what you are just imagining. So whatever you picture in your mind, your body will respond as if it is happening.

Whenever you have a thought, you release a chemical reaction that your body may feel. Plus, whatever images you put in your mind, you also release a chain reaction of emotions and impulses. In addition, your self-talk and ability to direct your mind can act like a steering wheel on that emotional roller coaster. Let's bring this information together using a real world example.

You decide to meet your spouse at a party, but after you arrived you cannot locate your spouse. Others begin to tell you that they have no idea where she or he is, or they tell you some wild and crazy ideas that just don't seem like your spouse. You continue to look, but cannot find she or he.

At this point, all sorts of thoughts begin flooding your mind along with crazy images of what might be going on. These thoughts and images are flooding your body with all sorts of emotional impulses and you begin to feel emotionally intoxicated. You are now riding the roller coaster! Finally, you find your spouse sitting by a fire all alone and everything is fine.

Now let's dissect this event. Once you began experiencing a flood of thoughts and images, your body responded accordingly and ratcheted up the emotions. In other words, the thoughts and images you were having are what ratcheted up the emotional roller coaster, not what was really happening. Remember, whatever you put into your mind is what is most real to you. Pretty much you are the one responsible for creating such an emotional roller coaster in this event by the way you were thinking and directing your mind in response to the event.

Whenever you are in a situation where you begin to experience the ratcheting up of the emotional roller coaster, you need to use your self-talk to steer and act like a director in your mind directing what the mind needs to focus upon.

In difficult situations, self-talk that helps soothe, remain in control, and that leads to a more empowering emotional response is what is needed. You also need to be a director and take control of what images you want your mind to see. Doing this will usually make the emotional roller coaster less intense and save your body from a slew of chemicals running through its veins.

First step is to begin to notice what your typical self-talk is like each day. Notice what you are telling yourself. Is it helpful or not? Then, begin to notice the images that stir up in your head. Are they helpful or not? Work to identify powerful self-talk and images that will release a more empowering emotional response that will aid you during difficult times.

LESSON SIXTEEN

DON'T LET YOURSELF BE EMOTIONALLY HIJACKED

LET'S NOT FORGET THAT THE LITTLE EMOTIONS ARE THE GREAT CAPTAINS OF OUR LIVES AND WE OBEY THEM WITHOUT REALIZING IT. – VINCENT VAN GOGH

16

DON'T LET YOURSELF BE EMOTIONALLY HIJACKED

You board an airplane destined for the great city of Chicago. Plane takes off and climbs to a comfortable cruising altitude of 30,000 feet. The plane ride has been pretty uneventful except for the arguing couple seated just behind you. Finally, the two quit arguing and the plane makes a successful landing. However, once you get out of the plane you realize you are NOT in Chicago, rather you are now in Anchorage, Alaska!

Take a few moments to think and reflect about this event before reading any further. What happened?

Hopefully you have never had to experience this unsettling event in your life. Then again, maybe you have, but not in the literal sense. What do I mean by that?

Have you ever told yourself with the utmost of determination that you were no longer going to eat that chocolate cake while on your diet but you did? How about your commitment to stick to your budget but somehow you gave-in and spent more than you had? Or, when you told yourself that you were no longer going to get mad and react to that awful coworker who gossips but, you found yourself reacting anyway! I could go on and on but, I think you get the point here.... Can you think of an example from your life?

You have pretty much set a goal with great motivation and determination but, when you try to accomplish the task, something happens. So, what is going on here? Quite simply, when you don't stop to think about your feelings and thoughts - including how they are influencing your behavior now and in the future – you are setting yourself up to be a frequent victim of emotional hijackings!

Whether you are aware of it or not, your emotions and thoughts will control you, and you'll move through the day reacting with little choice in what you say and do. In other words, the emotions and thoughts are piloting you and you have no idea!

Wouldn't it be nice if you had the skills necessary to deal with a hijacked plane successfully and safely? Sure, me too! I can't help you there, but I can give you two skill sets to work on to successfully deal with an emotional hijacking!

Self-awareness and Self-management are two core fundamental life skills needed to successfully navigate and prevent an emotional hijacking. When you learn to harness these two skills you have much better odds of managing you and ensuring mission success.

Self-awareness is the ability to read and understand yourself deep down below the surface. Your self-awareness is your radar of what is going on inside you! The more you work on improving your self-awareness, the better your radar is at picking up on what is going on inside.

Self-management is your ability to use awareness of your thoughts and emotions to actively choose what you say and do. Your self-management abilities are what keep you flying your plane on your chosen course and preventing any unwanted others from flying you!

Self-awareness and self-management are the one-two punch of reading yourself and then reacting in a way that keeps you in control.

When you are able to understand your thoughts and emotions and respond to them the way you choose, you then have the power to take control of difficult situations, deal with change easier, and take the initiative to achieve your goals!

It also ensures that you will no longer be getting in your own way and sabotaging your success (your own worst enemy). It will also limit the chances of you frustrating other people to the point they resent or dislike you.

If you would like to learn more about emotional hijackings, listen to the Don't Let Yourself Be Emotionally Hijacked episode on the Rhino Mentality Podcast.

LESSON SEVENTEEN

HAVE YOU EVER BEEN EMOTIONALLY INTOXICATED

WHEN DEALING WITH PEOPLE, REMEMBER YOU ARE NOT DEALING WITH CREATURES OF LOGIC, BUT CREATURES OF EMOTIONS. – DALE CARNEGIE

17

HAVE YOU EVER BEEN EMOTIONALLY INTOXICATED

I am quite sure you understand the effects of alcohol intoxication. Basically, your perceptions are altered, reaction time is slowed, you tend to do things you wouldn't normally do, heart rate is lowered, fine motor functioning is impaired and eventually gross motor functioning is impaired.

Pretty much you are unable to truly interpret what is going on around you and to function properly. Ever tried to have a discussion with someone who is intoxicated? How did that go? Have you ever been emotionally intoxicated? I can ask the same question, but in a different way…Have you ever had an emotionally charged conversation or argument with someone? Or, have you ever been emotionally worked up? If you answered yes, then you have been emotionally intoxicated!

It is important for you to understand what happens to you when you are, in a sense, emotionally intoxicated. First of all, it is much like being intoxicated with alcohol. Your perceptions are altered.

Pretty much you are seeing things through the lens of your emotions. Your heart rate is increasing, blood pressure increases, you may be slightly shaky as fine motor skills are reduced, your ability to listen to someone is greatly impaired, you develop selective hearing and attention, your insecurities and emotions begin to run the show, and you become quite reactive with limited ability to be rational and think before you speak!

You may have noticed this when you argued with someone. That person was not hearing the whole statement you were making and only heard certain words. Then, they began to twist your words and jump to conclusions. At this point, you may have become frustrated as this person is just not being rational. Or, that person could have been you!

You need to understand that when you are under the influence of your emotions and insecurities you are greatly impaired. You are not interpreting things accurately and are very prone to saying or doing things you may regret later.......sounds much like being intoxicated with alcohol huh?

Anyways, what is important is for you to develop awareness of when you have become too emotionally intoxicated or controlled by your emotions and insecurities. At the same time, you also need to develop awareness of when others have become too emotionally intoxicated. This skill is tremendously helpful for couples when engaged in an argument. Once they are able to recognize the signs of emotional intoxication they can take steps to ensure they do not do any further harm to the relationship.

Frankly, it doesn't take too much for emotions to begin to cloud your perceptions and impair your ability to function. However, there are four distinct behaviors that one exhibits when they are truly impaired. Watch out for these because when you notice them you are aware that this person is not interpreting your actions or words in a rational manner. Rather, they are misinterpreting. Or that person could be you!

Defensive.

Once a person becomes defensive they are no longer interested in hearing what you have to say. Rather, they are now in self-protective mode and will misinterpret your actions or words as attacks. In fact, they will only pay attention to certain words.

Overly critical.
A person who has become overly critical of you has now entered self-protective mode and is attacking as well. They are truly emotionally intoxicated and difficult to deal with in this state of mind.

Shut down (talk to the hand; or stonewall behavior).
If a person has shut down, they realize they are filled with way too much emotion and have chosen to just shut down. In a sense, they are essentially passed out! Continuing a conversation with this person will be of no benefit as they are overwhelmed and flooded in the brain. In fact, if you continue they may wake up and become more aggressive.

Condemning (name calling; belittling).
This is the person who is so emotionally intoxicated they are aggressive and dangerous. Do not waste time or energy engaging in a dialogue with such a person. They truly cannot hear you or even have the ability to have empathy for you at this point.

What to do?
If you find yourself or another in a state of emotional intoxication what can you do? Much like alcohol intoxication......they, or you, need time to sober up! Basically, it is time to calm down! Once you give it time, your senses and perceptions will return to normal (sobered up). But, watch out for the emotional hangover feelings of guilt, continued anger, difficulty sleeping, lowered appetite, nauseousness, headaches, fatigue, and irritability. Don't worry, they will go away and your senses will return again!

LESSON EIGHTEEN

HOW WELL DO YOU KNOW YOUR PARTNER

WHAT COUNTS IN MAKING A HAPPY MARRIAGE IS NOT SO MUCH HOW COMPATIBLE YOU ARE, BUT HOW YOU DEAL WITH INCOMPATIBILITY. – GEORGE LEVINGER

18

HOW WELL DO YOU KNOW YOUR PARTNER

Sally and Joe have gotten into another argument with each other; you know the one, the same one that keeps repeating over and over again.

Joe begins to feel overwhelmed and withdraws from the fight escaping into the bedroom and shuts the door. Joe does this often during a fight because to him calling a time out is the best thing to do before the argument gets too heated.

However, Sally becomes more outraged once Joe retreats and continues to follow him into the room. The fight continues and only escalates. Sally grew up with the idea that you need to talk it out no matter what and if you leave an argument that is the most disrespectful thing you could do. His retreating has now activated her fear of abandonment.

Sally and Joe continue to blame each other and try to prove the other person wrong; essentially, neither party is listening or seeking to understand the other. Soon both partners' insecurities are running the show. However, the couple has no idea or understanding of what is really going on.....how sad.

Couples that are able to weather through some of the most difficult marital challenges seem to possess the most intimate detailed map of their partner. In other words, they have worked to gain the most intimate deep details of their partner from how they respond to conflict to what their likes and dislikes are.

Without such knowledge you cannot "really" know your partner. And if you don't "really" know someone, how can you "truly" love them?

This knowledge of your partner not only leads to love but gives you a strong foundation to weather the nastiest of marital storms.

Let's look at a pretty common challenge in relationships, the birth of your first child. Research shows that 67% of couples will endure a dramatic decrease in marital satisfaction after the birth of their first child. However, the other 33% do not. In fact, half of the 33% actually showed an increase in marital satisfaction.

What's the difference between these two groups? The 33% had a solid understanding of each other. Not just a simple knowledge of their partner's likes and dislikes but, a real "deep" understanding of their partner's inner psychological world.

You need to have a solid understanding of your partner in order to weather the changes in your marital life. Having a child is just one of many possible changes. Loss of a job, moving, becoming grandparents, retiring, remarriage, stepfamilies, growth, death, and illness are just many other possibilities that can shake your relationship.

However, with a firm knowledge of your partner, you will be in a much better position to navigate the waters of change with little to no damage to the relationship. In fact, the changes may actually bring the two of you together even more!

Here are some suggestions to start:

1. Who are the cast of characters in my partner's life?
2. What are some recent important events in my partner's life?
3. What is my partner looking forward to? Dreading?
4. What are my partner's current stresses? Worries?
5. What are my partner's dreams and aspirations?
6. What are your partner's triumphs and successes?
7. What are your partner's psychological injuries and healings?
8. What is your partner's emotional world like? How does that interact with yours?

Answering such questions as a couple will lead to a greater understanding and intimacy than you could ever expect. This knowledge will help both of you understand each other and insulate your relationship against the trials and tribulations of marital life.

LESSON NINETEEN

FACING THE SUDDEN DEATH OF A LOVED ONE

WHILE GRIEF IS FRESH, EVERY ATTEMPT TO DIVERT ONLY IRRITATES. YOU MUST WAIT TILL IT BE DIGESTED, AND THEN AMUSEMENT WILL DISSIPATE THE REMAINS OF IT. – SAMUEL JOHNSON

19

FACING THE SUDDEN DEATH OF A LOVED ONE

When someone you know is going to die, you have a chance to prepare; at least a little. However, the unexpected and sudden death of a loved one can leave you feeling stunned, lost, and overwhelmed with pain. You may not even know where to begin to cope.

Sudden and unexpected loss of a loved one can be one of the most difficult events for anyone to deal with. Anytime you lose someone you love, whether it is sudden or not, it can be challenging. Sudden loss definitely provides a unique challenge as the shock can intensify and complicate the grief.

Sudden loss gives you no chance to prepare, leaves you feeling cheated as you never had the chance to say your goodbye's, and can make the world feel shaky and less safe while leaving you feeling fearful, uncertain, angry, and frustrated.

At some point in your life you will face the death of a loved one.

Cultivating fundamental beliefs that you believe to the very core of your soul will help you walk this difficult road.

The following is a list of key principles/beliefs to remember when dealing with sudden unexpected loss of a loved one and to deeply embed in the core of your soul as you prepare for such a difficult time:

1. **People do recover from sudden losses and you will too!** Grief is well known to mislead you into thinking that you will never recover. Don't buy this for one minute. It may be a tough road to walk, but as long as you continue walking you will recover.

2. **Love yourself and take special care of yourself while going through grief.** Grief is especially gifted at getting you to forget about taking care of yourself. Even remembering to eat and breathe can be difficult at times.

3. **Being strong and brave is important, but never, ever miss an opportunity to cry**. Dealing with your feelings in a sensible and honest way will help you to heal.

4. **Remember feelings expressed disappear; feelings repressed don't.** If I were to give you a hot rod of iron to hang onto, you would probably drop it immediately as it began to burn. So, don't hang on to those feelings as those will burn too!

5. **Get some support and teammates.** Seek out a counselor, support group, church group, or any other supportive relationship or group. Walking a road of grief by yourself can be deadly; seek out teammates that can help you along the way.

6. **The person you lost would want you to recover from losing them.** This is a very critical belief to adopt even before you lose someone close to you. Hang on to this belief tight!

7. **The person you lost would want you to remember and honor them by living a fulfilling life.** Grief is tough. You will have some really tough days and nights, but give it your best shot at living and creating a fulfilling life as this can be one of the most honorable ways to remember and honor them.

If you are going through a sudden loss of a loved one please remember these critical items as they can help you heal. However, if you know of someone who is going through such a loss then also keep these in mind as you can become a very valuable teammate for them to heal.

LESSON TWENTY

HOW TO STRENGTHEN YOUR PSYCHOLOGICAL CORE

FALL SEVEN TIMES, STAND UP EIGHT. – JAPANESE PROVERB

20

HOW TO STRENGTHEN YOUR PSYCHOLOGICAL CORE

Gaining physical core strength is absolutely essential because your physical core is the vital foundation of all of your body's movements. Whether you are walking, running, carrying something, or whatever, all of these movements are a direct result of your core strength.

It is virtually the same thing when it comes to psychological strength. Your psychological core is the vital foundation that drives your behavior and responses to life. Essentially, it is much like building a house; you need a solid foundation to build upon. Your psychological core is that foundation from which you build your life upon!

Three of the main components of your psychological core are your values, beliefs, and your sense of purpose. Your values are simply your principles and standards that can be summed up in one word. For example, honor, humor, honesty, etc....

Your beliefs are what you believe in and can be summed up in a brief statement or quotation. For instance, "where there's a will, there's a way," "hard work pays off," or "don't ever give up."

A sense of purpose is the "why" of what you are doing. It answers the question, "why is this important to you?" For example, if you have a goal of losing weight and keeping it off, your purpose (or why) is what will get you through those hard challenging times and keep you on the right track. Your sense of purpose can range from a life purpose to a goal-specific purpose like the example above.

Now that you are aware of what makes up your psychological core, let me give you some specific exercises you can do to build and strengthen that foundation you are building your precious life upon.

1. **Identify your life's purpose** – This task definitely takes time and is important to continue to revise as your life evolves. Find a quiet place to sit, and ponder upon the question of what in life is really important to you? As you reflect, write down what comes up. Then, ask yourself what do I want to be known as or what do I want to be known for? Again, write down what comes up. After engaging in these tasks, try to summarize up what you have written down into one sentence beginning with "my life's purpose is." For example, my life's purpose is to learn, grow, strengthen myself, inspire, love, and enjoy life.

2. **Identify your values** – You want to identify values you want to guide your life. For this task, go to google and type in "quotes." Pick any of the quotations pages from the list and you should usually see an "A to Z" listing of quotations under certain words. Use the long list of A to Z words and begin to choose words you would like to be guided by. Narrow the list to 10. Once accomplished, you now have identified values you would like to be guided by.

3. **List of Beliefs** – Once again, you can go to the quotations pages and begin to collect various quotes that you like. You can start by collecting quotes under your values. As time goes, you will be

collecting a number of empowering beliefs. This list will help to serve you during some difficult times.

There you have it, three simple exercises you can do to begin to strengthen your psychological core. Keep your results near and dear to your heart during times of challenge. Begin to program these results into your mind daily!

LESSON TWENTY-ONE

WHAT THE "LION KING" CAN TEACH YOU ABOUT LIFE

OH YES, THE PAST CAN HURT. BUT THE WAY I SEE IT, YOU CAN EITHER RUN FROM IT, OR...LEARN FROM IT. – RAFIKI, FROM THE MOVIE LION KING

21

WHAT THE "LION KING" CAN TEACH YOU ABOUT LIFE

Many of us have enjoyed the Walt Disney Classic "The Lion King." For me, the movie brings back memories of sitting around the television with my wife and kids and laughing at the crazy antics of Timon and Pumba.

Do you remember this movie? Simba, the main character is tricked into thinking he had killed his father. So he flees away from his homeland and tries to forget all about his past identity as the future King. Eventually, Simba comes to term with his past and returns to his pride land to find it in shambles. He battles his uncle and the hyenas in order to reclaim his land and rescue the pride.

That description may be a little bleak as the movie has a great deal more to it. Anyhow, what does this movie teach you about life? Do you remember the scene where Simba is cracked over the head with a big stick by that crazy monkey Rafiki who spoke with a Jamaican accent?

In that scene, Simba states, I *know what I have to do. But going back means I'll have to face my past. I've been running from it for so long.*" "Rafiki then cracks Simba over the head with a big stick and Simba exclaims, "*Ow...what was that for?*" Rafiki then replies and laughs, "*It doesn't matter, it is in the past*" To which Simba then returns, "*Yeah, but it still hurts!*" Then comes some wise words from Rafiki when he exclaims, "*Oh yes, the past can hurt. But the way I see it, you can either run from it, or...learn from it.*"

That's the life teaching scene! Do you understand? You see Rafiki was simply helping Simba take personal accountability for his life. No matter what has happened in the past, it is just that.....the past! There is nothing you can ever do about the past. No matter how angry or how emotional you get about the past, it NEVER changes the past. But it will still hurt.

What matters most is "What are you going to do about it now? Or, "How are you going to respond to it now?" That you have control over! You do not have control over anything in your past but, you do have control over how you respond to it now!

Anytime you use "What" or "How" questions you begin to reclaim control over the impact of your past and begin to focus upon solutions that you can use in that very moment to limit the pain of your past.

If you want to lessen the pain of the past, then simply STOP thinking about it consistently. Whenever you think about such past pains, you are in essence feeding this pain to grow on within you. First, catch yourself dwelling on it. Second distract your thinking by focusing upon something else. Continue this process whenever the mind tries to think about the past again.

LESSON TWENTY-TWO

HOW BLAMING CAN TAKE AWAY YOUR POWER

THE TENDENCY TO WHINING AND COMPLAINING MAY BE TAKEN AS THE SUREST SIGN SYMPTOM OF LITTLE SOULS AND INFERIOR INTELLECTS. – LORD JEFFREY

22

HOW BLAMING CAN TAKE AWAY YOUR POWER

"He made me do it." "My whole day is wrecked because of you!" My life is wrecked because of this!" If my husband could just do this I would feel so much better."

Have you ever heard statements like these? I know I have both heard them and probably used similar phrases at some point during my life.

If you are honest with yourself you may admit that you too have used such statements in the past. Nobody's perfect not even myself. Just because I am a therapist and writing this lesson doesn't mean that I am better than you or more perfect. I am human just like anybody else.

So, what is the problem with such statements anyways? I mean most people tend to use such statements nearly every day, so what is the problem? Maybe there isn't anything really wrong with such statements and we therapists just need to find problems.

You see, you give away your power when you use such statements! When you say, "He made me do it." Essentially you have handed over your power to him and now his actions or statements control you. Wow what power you gave to him! All he has to do is say this or do that and you just do it as if you had no mind of your own!

"My whole day is wrecked because of you!" REALLY! Why would you hand over your whole day to someone that upset you? You may feel upset and angry but that doesn't mean that the rest of the day is gone! Again you have given up your power to feel better and empowered this other person to control how you feel the rest of the day! Wow how easily you give up your power.

"If my husband could just do this I would feel so much better." In this statement, you have given up the power for you to feel better and placed it in someone else's hands. In a sense, now you get to gamble and just hope that this person does something. Otherwise, you are going to be miserable. Why put the power to control your emotional life in the hands of someone else? If you do, then you better hope they are pretty normal otherwise you could be in trouble!

Many times I hear from people that if certain people and circumstances could finally get it and change that their lives would be so much better. This creates a sense of hopelessness because with such beliefs you have no power over changing and feeling better. It is now up to circumstances and many others to change just so you can feel better! Plus, your emotional life is now in the hands of the up and down world. Guess how you just might feel? If you guessed "up and down," then you guessed right!

Why wait? Take back your power by demonstrating better self-accountability and being honest with yourself. If someone did something to wreck your day, then admit that you are feeling like that because you are choosing to hand over your day to them. STOP! Admit that your day is wrecked because YOU have chosen that in response to whatever someone did. You don't have to choose that! You can choose to feel the way you want to. Just because this or that happens does not mean you have to feel lousy for the rest of the day or your life for that matter! You take back your power to choose and then decide how you want to respond. We cannot control others or circumstances but we can control how we RESPOND to them!

Now I am not perfect and even I find myself struggling with this at times. It seems that it is easier and feels good to blame others for your circumstances and lot in life. However, if you really want to change that then you must take back your power by realizing that you have CHOSEN to respond this way. And then CHOOSE a different response, CHOOSE to focus or dwell on something else, CHOOSE to look at the problem in a different way that leads to changing your feelings, or CHOOSE to simply let it go. Some things are not that important when we compare them to life and death situations!

After reading this, do you have any thoughts or comments about this? What other examples might you say others use to give away their power? In what ways have you fallen prey to giving away your power? What ways can you use to take back your power? Remember it is in our choices that we can recover our power!

Your challenge is to first seek to understand this lesson, then go out and begin living it! I challenge you to go at least one day without blaming, complaining, or whining.

LESSON TWENTY-THREE

HOW A SIMPLE GESTURE CAN SAVE SOMEONE'S LIFE

BE KIND WHENEVER POSSIBLE. IT IS ALWAYS POSSIBLE. – TENZIN GYATSO, 14TH DALAI LAMA

23

HOW A SIMPLE GESTURE CAN SAVE SOMEONE'S LIFE

What you are about to read is based on a true story but, the names have been changed to ensure confidentiality.

Joe was a young man who was brought up with much difficulty in his life. In fact, his mother had died when he was young and he was raised by his alcoholic father.

Joe was in his early twenties, struggling to make financial ends meet, and felt as though no one ever seemed to notice him. It seemed each time I met with him he would talk about how people would just pass right on by him without even acknowledging him in any way. He felt like he was invisible and dead to the world.

One day, he made a very fateful decision. He decided that he would enter a grocery store, go to the chips aisle, and if the next person who passes him by doesn't acknowledge him in any way, then he is going to kill himself.

So, he went into the grocery store, went to the chips aisle, and waited for a person to walk by.

Sally was a middle aged woman from a fairly decent home who was currently raising her three children all by herself as her husband had passed away a few years ago. Upon his passing, she seemed to distance herself from others and kept to herself quite a bit.

Sally's youngest child loved sour cream and onion potato chips. She decided to stop off at the local grocery store, buy some of those chips, and surprise her daughter later.

That day, Sally had no idea that a man was waiting in the chips aisle and would kill himself if the next person to pass him didn't acknowledge him in any way; Sally was going to be this person. She had no idea that in that moment she held the power to save someone's life!

Sally entered the chips aisle and saw a man standing there. As she passed him, she simply gave him a nod and nothing else.

Joe, noticing the nod, decided not to kill himself and from that day forward worked to improve his life and never again considered to kill himself. In fact, he went on to live a pretty fulfilling life upon completion of his counseling with me.

How many times have we passed by others without even acknowledging them in any way? Sally had no idea how much control she had over Joe's life in that moment and how a simple nod set the stage for a great turnaround for Joe.

Many times, we are so focused upon ourselves that we do not acknowledge those around us. Sometimes, it is even children that we do not acknowledge. I would like to invite you all to examine and notice how often you acknowledge others. And remember, each and every one of us is important and valued in some way. No matter the shortcomings or failures, our humanity as a human being is always worthy of acknowledgment.

LESSON TWENTY-FOUR

DANGER! STOP IGNORING YOUR BODY'S ALERT SYSTEM

THE GREATEST WEALTH IS HEALTH - VIRGIL

24

DANGER! STOP IGNORING YOUR BODY'S ALERT SYSTEM

I am sure you understand that if the check engine light in your vehicle lights up that it is alerting you to a potential problem. It is then advisable to discontinue driving the vehicle and get it checked out pretty quick.

But what if you just dismantle the fuse that lights up the check engine light? Then, the light will go away and it will not be alerting you every time you drive the vehicle. However, with the light now off, does that mean that the problem with the vehicle is gone as well?

That is a pretty silly question to think the problem is gone just because you deactivate the check engine light. In fact, you would think I am crazy if I actually believed that the problem is now gone because you just simply deactivated the light, right?

Then why do you seek to deactivate your body's alert system when it is only trying to let you know that you are experiencing a problem? What do I mean by that exactly? Let's look at an example of stress.

How can you tell if you are experiencing stress? Well, your body begins to show signs of fatigue; you experience muscle tension, headaches, eyes become tired, stomach pains or even heartburn, difficulty concentrating, and simply a feeling of being overloaded. Now I know there are many more symptoms but, this is just a quick list for this simple example.

These signs are your body's check engine lights! They are alerting you to potential problems. There are numerous emotional and physical disorders that have been linked to stress including depression, anxiety, heart attacks, stroke, hypertension, immune system disturbances that increase susceptibility to infections. In fact, it's hard to think of any disease in which stress did not play a role or any part of the body that is not affected.

So why do you deactivate your body's alert system by ignoring or masking these issues? Instead of listening to them, you may decide to take some aspirin to cover up that headache, maybe some muscle relaxers to loosen the muscles, some heartburn pills to deal with the heartburn, pour some coffee or other type of caffeine to keep us going, use alcohol or drugs, smoking cigarettes, and even put Visine in your eyes to get the red out! This list of how you may mask or deal with the symptoms of stress, and not seek to get at the root of the problem, can go on and on.

It's crazy to think you can just dull your senses to stress and then continue to run your body's engine at full power without any problems! I guess you just need to learn the hard way and wait till you experience one of those heart attacks, strokes, depression, and so on before you finally get it!

Instead, start listening to how your body is reacting during the day. Then adjust how you are coming at the day or dealing with the day to help alleviate the stress. Certainly taking an aspirin or whatever from time to time is not bad, it is only bad when you are chronically doing that.

Try engaging in some deep breathing for 5 minutes a few times throughout the day rather than smoke that cigarette. In fact, it is not the cigarette that calms you; it is the way you are breathing when smoking that actually calms you!

Or, prepare your body to deal with such stress by strengthening your mental and physical realms. Start by exercising and eating healthy. Couple that with working to create more positive self-talk and creating more empowering emotions or feelings rather than those toxic feelings and thoughts you might be saturated with daily.

Quite simply, you cannot continue to deal with stress the same way. You need to start adjusting your responses to your body's natural check engine lights. If you need some help, seek out a counselor who can help.

LESSON TWENTY-FIVE

ARE YOUR INSECURITIES BRAINWASHING YOU?

PROGRESS ALWAYS INVOLVES RISKS. YOU CAN'T STEAL SECOND BASE AND KEEP YOUR FOOT ON FIRST. – FREDERICK B. WILCOX

25

ARE YOUR INSECURITIES BRAINWASHING YOU?

You're sitting at work when all of the sudden a bunch of gunmen break in and take you captive. The captors remove you and place you in isolation and then begin the tactics of brainwashing. First off they will usually prey upon your fears and increasing your anxiety to an intolerable panic coupled with not allowing you to sleep. You will begin to feel extreme discomfort, sleep deprivation, and it will be a matter of time before you are feeling broken down.

At some point during this breaking down phase, they also begin to launch an assault on your identity. Telling you things like, "You are nothing," "you are no good," and "who do you think you are." They also repeatedly attack you at your psychological base by hammering away at your beliefs and values. Eventually you are in extreme discomfort and broken down.

At some point, they switch tactics and begin to offer you a way out of the suffering. This way out is usually if you do what they want you to do and believe what they want you to believe. Soon you give in and begin a life in captivity. Staying within the captive walls and dreaming of what it would be like to be on the outside.

Not many of us have ever experienced being in captivity or brainwashing to this extent. However, what if I told you that being captive and brainwashed is quite common? You would probably think I was nuts! The truth is we are all held captive and brainwashed into our comfort zones by our insecurities all the time!

Think about it. We stay within the walls of our comfort zone dreaming about a better relationship, more money, that dream job, and simply the life we really want to live.

At times, you get motivated, set some goals and begin that quest to achieve the life you really want. Soon you are near the walls of the comfort zone and anxiety begins to set off its bells and whistles leaving you feeling discomfort while getting more uncomfortable as you continue to approach the barrier.

Soon after, fear steps in and begins to put all sorts of images in your head of what might happen if you continue; images of failure, humiliation, pain, and regret. You begin to feel fright and panic. At that point, doubt sets in and begins a barrage of shaming you to the core by questioning your very identity, actions, and behaviors.

Soon it begins to appear like it is too much to continue and insecurity offers you some respite if you just stop the journey and head back to the illusion of the safety and security within the captive walls of your comfort zone. Then comes even more internal shaming and assault on your core beliefs and identity as you quit the journey to a life you really desired.

The truth is that there is no real safety and security behind your comfort zone, only the feeling of captivity. If you really want the life you dreamed of, then you need to move the barrier of your comfort zone back. Doing so means facing the experience above.

Have you ever set a goal and didn't achieve it? Have you ever had the experience where you knew what you needed to do but didn't do it? Think about your attempts to get out of debt, have a great marriage, lose that weight, etc. How successful were you?

The challenge you miss and do not prepare for is the battle with the insecurities as you stretch your comfort zone and seek out those goals. The key to success and staying in the fight is your level of emotional mastery! Emotional mastery is your ability to manage your emotional experience in the direction you are seeking rather than having it use you!

If you want the life you dreamed of then I challenge you today to begin to learn about emotional mastery. Look it up on Google and begin reading about it, then begin to put it in action! It is simple, but never easy!

LESSON TWENTY-SIX

YOU CAN CHOOSE TO GROW WEEDS OR FLOWERS

LIFE IS WHAT WE MAKE IT, ALWAYS HAS BEEN, ALWAYS WILL BE – GRANDMA MOSES

26

YOU CAN CHOOSE TO GROW WEEDS OR FLOWERS

Many times in life you may be subjected to other people's negative comments or actions. Pretty much, you find that others, at times, will say and do something that just absolutely triggers a very uncomfortable, sticky, smelly, emotional storm inside of you. When that happens, they have just spread the manure.

Once the manure is spread, one of two things will happen. Either you will make the choice to live in the weeds that will sprout, or you will make a flower from this. What do I mean by all this manure, weeds, and flowers?

Let's take an example. On 9/11 we were all subjected to a very large spreading of manure when a tragic act of terrorism took place. After this event many of us felt an enormous emotional storm inside that left us feeling pretty (place expletive here that also describes manure, lol).

From this manure of emotions sprouted a great deal of negative hateful thoughts and behaviors; these are the weeds. These negative hateful thoughts and behaviors can take over your life and get you to become something you are not. In other words, this event spirals you into negativity and darkness as the weeds continue to grow.

However, many of us choose to weed ourselves of that negativity, began to make a flower, and let the terrorists know that they cannot control or terrorize our lives by their manure and weeds!

Flowers have grown as evidenced by the numbers of young people flocking to the military, the patriotism that has fostered, and the coming together of a nation along with many other positive aspects.

How does this relate to you and your life? Simply, throughout your life you will experience a great deal of crappy events or statements made by other people. When you have those crappy times, and you will feel crappy inside, you must remember that such crap will fertilize weeds or flowers. The choice is yours in which you want to control your life.

The process is simple, manure is spread. You feel crappy and it just stinks! From these events weeds will fester within your mind and your life, making it real tough to experience great joy and happiness. However, if you decide to grow, learn, or use the event then you will grow flowers and rid yourself of the weeds and the stench of manure. Then you finally begin to smell the greatness of beautifully grown flowers!

So, the next time you are experience a manure spreading, the choice is yours! Live in the weeds and stench, or find a way to grow flowers from this and make a difference in the lives of others. Remember, the choice is always yours!

LESSON TWENTY-SEVEN

MAKING MISTAKES IS NOT AN OPTION, IT IS ESSENTIAL!

WHILE ONE PERSON HESITATES BECAUSE HE FEELS INFERIOR, THE OTHER IS BUSY MAKING MISTAKES AND BECOMING SUPERIOR. – HENRY C. LINK

27

MAKING MISTAKES ARE NOT AN OPTION, IT IS ESSENTIAL!

Mistakes are a normal part of everyone's life. You learn from your own mistakes and from the mistakes of others. Mistakes will teach you about yourself, your limitations, and where you need to work to get better.

What is important is for you to realize that mistakes do happen and they are a gateway to learning. In fact, successful individuals will state one of the reasons for their success was they were able to overcome more mistakes than most people can handle.

Not only do you learn from mistakes but, also from observations of others. In fact, our children tend to learn from this way a great deal! If you don't think they are paying attention to how you respond to mistakes, then you are greatly mistaken!

So what is your lesson in this mistake? To stop reading this and begin denial? Or, to read on and enjoy the adventure of learning?

When your child spills their cereal on the floor (and this WILL happen). Or, if you are a coach, and your players screw up. How do you respond? Certainly, they have made a mistake and need to learn not to do this again. But, the lesson here is about your approach and how you may be indirectly teaching them about mistakes. What might that mean ("that" meaning indirectly teaching them)?

You see, they need to learn not to repeat the mistake of spilling food on the floor or making that inadvertent pass on the basketball court (but then again they are only human as you are). However, through observation they are indirectly learning how to treat someone that has made a mistake!

Have you ever made a mistake in your life? How would you want the other person to treat you? Do you react to other's mistakes like that? Are you teaching that to your children?

Great leaders understand the principle of the Golden Rule which is to treat others as you wish to be treated. Don't forget that the child you are trying to teach is a developing young person who has thoughts and feelings as you do. Please try to not treat them like an object.

Through observation they are also learning about how to overcome a mistake. Are you modeling that to your children as well? By badgering and taking your anger out on them, you are damaging that young person's sense of who they are and what they are capable of. The lower this is, the less likely they may feel confident in the future to overcome mistakes (which makes it more likely they will do it again).

Most people using this approach feel that by letting them see how angry they have become it will deter them from doing it again. But, if their mistake is only because they are human, then you are indirectly teaching them they have to be perfect to get your love! Is that what you desire? Are you perfect? Have you ever done what they did?

The lesson here is simple but not easy to do. Learn to pay more attention at the indirect effects of your actions around others. If you don't want them yelling at you, then don't yell at them. If you don't want them being critical of you, then stop being so critical of them. If you want them to develop compassion, then you must demonstrate compassion.

It is a simple formula by just filling in the blank: If you want them to _____ then you must demonstrate _____. If you don't want them to do _____ then don't do _____ to them.

Remember that in order to learn or get better you must make mistakes. In fact, mistakes are essential to success. You need to mistake your way to success!

There are other lessons being indirectly taught with mistakes. Can you identify some others?

LESSON TWENTY-EIGHT

AN IMPORTANT LESSON THAT JUST MIGHT SAVE YOUR LIFE

TO CONQUER FRUSTRATION, ONE MUST REMAIN INTENSELY FOCUSED ON THE OUTCOME, NOT THE OBSTACLES. – T.F. HODGE

28

AN IMPORTANT LESSON THAT JUST MIGHT SAVE YOUR LIFE

Do you remember the biblical story of Jesus walking on the water? If not, let me recap for you. Please keep in mind that I am not a biblical scholar nor was I alive when this happened. In other words, I may be paraphrasing a bit or missing some details.

Anyhow, within this event contains a very powerful principle about living your life; especially during times of struggle and chaos. Some of Jesus' disciples were on a boat crossing a body of water when they looked up and noticed that Jesus was approaching them by walking on the water. Jesus then asked one of the disciples to get out of the boat and also walk on the water. So, the disciple got out and began to walk on the water. Much to his amazement, the disciple began to look down at his feet and then began to sink. Jesus told the disciple to keep his eyes firmly focused on Jesus. Once the disciple did this, he began to walk on the water again.

So, what is the life lesson in this great powerful story? It is lesson for you to remember to pay attention to what you are focusing on when going through difficulties. When faced with a crisis many begin to focus upon the craziness that is going on around them. When you do this, the inevitable result is that you begin to lose your power and strength needed to overcome the obstacle; essentially you begin to sink.

Rather, you need to focus upon a source of strength and the actions needed to overcome. Only then you will regain the strength and power needed to overcome. Just like the disciple who changed his focus back to Jesus and then continued to walk on the water.

When you are essentially going through hell in your life it is easy to begin to focus upon all the crap that is going on around you. You begin to focus and draw your attention to the scariness of what is happening in your life. This results in creating a mindset of panic and overwhelm. You will never find your strength and the way out when in this mindset.

Simply catch yourself focusing on these things. Identify something that gives you strength and then focus only upon the actions needed to overcome. Remember, when you are going through hell don't stop and look at all the crazy sites around you. Keep focused on your plan of getting out and identify a source of strength and you may find yourself overcoming the odds and getting through the difficulty.

Facing difficulties is tough on your own. The problems of our life are aware of this. We are stronger in numbers. Therefore, it is important to identify some teammates or supports to help you during this difficult time. I would recommend visiting with a counselor to help guide and support you through the challenge.

LESSON TWENTY-NINE

WHAT YOU MUST KNOW ABOUT EMOTIONAL RESILIENCE

LIFE DOESN'T GET EASIER OR MORE FORGIVING; WE GET STRONGER AND MORE RESILIENT. – STEVE MARABOLI

29

WHAT YOU MUST KNOW ABOUT EMOTIONAL RESILIENCE

I am pretty sure you understand that to attain life's goals and dreams you need to be totally committed, driven to succeed, set good goals, and never ever quit!

You can be totally committed and driven to succeed and think that you will never quit or fail, but if you are emotionally weak you will quit and fail every time! It doesn't matter how much you think about not quitting or failing, you are still going to quit and fail.

Maybe your goal was to lose weight, gain a promotion, stay married, get married, find a job, deal with depression and anxiety, remain clean of drugs, etc. Whatever the goal was, eventually you set good goals, committed yourself to those goals, and began the journey to accomplish them.

At some point in the journey you were met with challenges and frustrations. Things didn't go quite the way you expected them too. Progress wasn't quite happening, or it wasn't as fast as you wanted it to. You may have begun to experience pains and frustrations. You began to become overwhelmed and stressed.

At this point, you may have become angry at yourself or others; maybe felt some pity. Eventually you began looking for a way out and began to make catastrophic choices that only resulted in more frustration. You were now headed straight forward on the road to quit and fail!

No one said life would be easy. In fact, any goal worthy of attaining will have grand challenges and frustrations that we all need to overcome in order to succeed. Mental Toughness is only half the equation. Emotional resiliency is the other!

Emotional resilience is the ability to adapt to stressful situations or crises. One component of emotional resilience is self-control. Self-control is the capacity to manage strong emotions and impulses rather than give into them; in other words, the ability to handle troublesome emotions.

As indicated previously, if you are emotionally weak you will quit and fail every time. The minute you start facing difficulty, a swarm of emotions comes up, you get frustrated or angry, and look to fail or sabotage your success.

Sheer willpower is not enough! You can continue to press on with tremendous willpower, but if you cannot manage those emotions and impulses you will fail and quit every time.

Developing emotional resilience or emotional strength allows you to face those difficult and strong emotions, process them, and reduce the impact of those emotions. Therefore, continuing the course towards your goals rather than beginning to crumble!

You truly are your own worst enemy. However, you can also become your greatest ally by developing your ability to manage emotions. Learn to manage your internal world first, and then you will begin to see the outer success you are looking for.

If you would love to learn more about developing emotional resilience, then check out <u>Rhino Mentality Podcast – Episode Mental Toughness Tools – Emotional Resilience</u>.

LESSON THIRTY

IF YOU CAN MANAGE A POP BOTTLE, YOU CAN MANAGE YOUR EMOTIONS

SPEAK WHEN YOU ARE ANGRY AND YOU WILL MAKE THE BEST SPEECH YOU WILL EVER REGRET.
– AMBROSE BIERCE

30

IF YOU CAN MANAGE A POP BOTTLE, YOU CAN MANAGE YOUR EMOTIONS

Do you drink soda pop or know someone who does? What if I shook up a bottle and handed it to you to open right here without it going all over the place? How might you do that?

You might let it sit for a while. You might loosen the cap letting out some pressure while watching the suds rise and closing the cap at just the right moment. Or, you may find a sink or safe place to let the bottle open and explode.

You and I are much like a pop bottle. When things happen in life we get shook up! And if we do not manage that pressure building, then we will blow up like the pop bottle and leave a really sticky mess for everyone around us.

Simply put, you can use the same advice needed to manage a shook-up pop bottle in order to manage your emotions. Take a minute and think about it…

When you feel that pressure building you could take a break and sit quietly for a while until the pressure subsides. This is no different than just letting the shook up pop bottle sit for a bit.

Or, you could vent a bit but, don't let the pressure get too high before you close your cap! Much like opening the bottle slightly, releasing some pressure, but keeping an eye on the fizz so it doesn't overflow!

What are some ways you can slowly release some pressure in your life?

Sometimes the bottle is too shook up and is exploding. Then, you need to find a safe place for it to release; a sink for example. If the pressure is too high and you are going to blow, then find a safe place to vent so there is no sticky emotional mess. You could always find a field and scream, find a place to yourself, scream in a pillow, etc. Can you think of other ideas?

Probably the biggest key to any successful endeavor is managing your emotions. If you are able to manage a pop bottle then you can manage your emotions. Whatever method you choose to manage your emotions, the first step is always recognizing the buildup of those emotions.

Awareness is critical and requires your concentration. It is easy to visually see the fizz rising in a pop bottle, but more of a challenge for you to sense the fizzy buildup within yourself; this takes practice.

The key is to just remember to check your emotional buildup throughout the day so you don't unknowingly explode all over yourself or others.

Managing your emotions can be as simple as managing a pop bottle. However, as humans we tend to make things more difficult than they need to be.

Take the time to identify some ways to slowly release some pressure throughout the day; then begin to do them daily. Don't forget to find some quiet still time to settle down. Oh, and definitely locate a safe place when the emotional fizz is just too much to bear!

LESSON THIRTY-ONE

TALE OF TWO BROTHERS AND A SECRET YOU MUST KNOW

I AM THE MASTER OF MY FATE; I AM THE CAPTAIN OF MY SOUL. – FROM INVICTUS BY WILLIAM ERNEST HENLEY

31

TALE OF TWO BROTHERS AND A SECRET YOU MUST KNOW

Many years ago I read or heard a story about two twin brothers which contained an enormous life lesson that many need to know. This life lesson is one of the core beliefs of being a "Rhino" and developing a Rhino Mentality.

The two brothers were identical twins and raised by an abusive alcoholic father. Their father not only greatly abused alcohol, but tortured and tormented the brothers physically, verbally, and emotionally for years.

Many years later, an individual was greatly intrigued by the success of one of the brothers and sought out a chance to interview him. This individual wanted to know what this brother attributed his success to.

When asked directly, the brother replied, "I had to find a way up and out. My alcoholic father terribly abused my brother and I when we were kids. I knew that if I didn't work hard and seek a better life, that I would end up just like my father."

The interviewer was amazed and began to wonder about how the other brother turned out and what he would attribute such a life to. So, the interviewer began the process of tracking him down.

The other brother was eventually found to be homeless and living in the streets as a bum. The interviewer asked "What do you attribute your bad situation and luck to?" This brother replied, "I had no choice. My alcoholic father terribly abused my brother and I when we were kids. I didn't stand a chance."

The moral of this story is that you are the "author" of your life not the "object." You have the ability to write the story of your life. Do not let anyone else or your circumstances control your destiny!

You must believe that you have a choice to be in control of your life. To be the author and write the story as you see fit, rather than just being acted upon by circumstances and others. It is not what happened to you that matters most, it is how you decide to respond to life that determines your eventual outcomes.

Begin today to take charge of your responses and choices towards life. Then you will have the opportunity to create the life you desire and deserve. But remember, it all begins with the belief that you are the "author" with the ability to write the story of your life, and not the "object" and simply at the mercy of circumstances and others!

LESSON THIRTY-TWO

TIME TO START ENJOYING YOUR LIFE

LIFE IS MEANT TO BE ENJOYED. – MARVIN DAUNER (MY GRANDFATHER)

32

TIME TO START ENJOYING YOUR LIFE

We seem to live in a fast-paced society, always on the go, and having too many things to do in one day. In fact, if your to-do list is like mine, you find that you have plenty of items listed, but limited time to get them all done.

Each day, there can be numerous instances that compete for your attention. Then you clutter the mind even more when you begin to think about all the upcoming things you need to attend to. You would think you would just stop there, but no, you need to keep overwhelming your mind. So, you start thinking about events in your life that upset you or happened yesterday or even longer ago. Then you start to wonder why you are so overwhelmed, tired, fatigued, have headaches, irritable, and just can't seem to enjoy life!

With all these things going on in your mind, you are pretty much breaking yourself down and creating more problems than need be. In fact, an airplane will only use full power when taking off because to continue to do so would pretty much burn up the engine and a hard resounding crash would soon approach! You ever had a mental crash or catastrophe?

Overwhelming yourself and cluttering your mind prevents you from being able to enjoy the moment, cherish your times with loved ones, and to simply just feel free. You seem to be physically located in the moment, but mentally are definitely not on board. Life is too short to waste even a precious moment.

My favorite book of all time is Walden written by the great Henry David Thoureau. I feel this book is a must read for everyone because it contains so many valuable lessons. See the list below for a just a few of those lessons and see how it might apply to your life:

1. Keep it simple. Learn to simplify your life. There is never any benefit to make a situation any more complex than it needs to be. Plus, there is no grand reward to clutter your schedule at the cost of the quality of time spent with those you care about most.

2. Learn to appreciate the finer things in life. When spending time with those you care about most, be sure to soak up every minute in your mind like a camera might. Record every feeling, taste, smell, touch, and sound in detail. Truly be observant and describe in minute detail the experience like Thoureau describes Walden pond.

3. Stay in the moment. You may be physically with your loved one, but emotionally and mentally you are elsewhere when your mind is cluttered. Work to be as present in the moment as you can.

4. Learn to let go of the clutter. At least let it go for the moment. Don't worry about losing it, because it will wait for you. Once you have left the moment it will be right there waiting for you with a bright shiny smile.

Life is precious and needs to be treated as such. The time and relationships you develop in your lifetime are what truly matters most. Be sure to keep this in mind.

ABOUT THE AUTHOR

Chris Swenson is an individual that truly operates his life with a "Rhino Mentality" – Powerful, meaning strong, wise, and resilient! He is a Licensed Marriage and Family Therapist in the state of Colorado. He owns and operates his own private practice, Rhino Wellness Center. He has dedicated his life to helping others navigate the waters of life. He lives with his wife and three children in Colorado.

Check out Rhino Wellness Center:
http://rhinowellnesscenter.com

Check out Rhino Mentality Podcast (found on iTunes)
http://apple.co/2vurEct

Contact Chris:
chriss@rhinowellnesscenter.com

Made in the USA
Coppell, TX
22 August 2023

20653805R00111